Reflections and Homilies: The Gonzaga Connection

By William M. Watson, S.J.

Wipf & Stock
PUBLISHERS
Eugene, Oregon

Wipf and Stock publishers
199 W 8th Ave, Suite 3
Eugene, OR 97401

Reflections and Homilies: The Gonzaga Connection
By William M. Watson
Edited by Dale Goodwin

ISBN: 1-59752-213-9

Copy Reader: Peter Tormey
Layout and Cover Design: Sandy Hank

About the Author

William Watson entered the Society of Jesus in 1973. He earned his undergraduate degree in philosophy at Gonzaga University and his graduate degree in Theology at The Weston Jesuit School of Theology. For 25 years he has created retreat programs for high schools, universities, and corporate executives. He served as Georgetown University's first Director of Retreat Programs where over 12 years he established a new national standard for university retreat programming. In 1999 he became Gonzaga University's first Vice President for Mission and founded 15 major programs and initiatives in the Roman Catholic, Jewish, and Protestant traditions. Paulist Press recently published a book of his on spirituality. Currently he serves as the Oregon Province Assistant for Colombia and International Ministries and is beginning a doctorate in ministry at the Catholic University of America.

Dedication

Many significant people were responsible for the successful development of Gonzaga University's new ministry programs after I became Vice President for Mission in 1999. This collection of reflections and homilies is dedicated to just some of them.

I would like to remember all the Gonzaga Trustees, in particular Dave and Sandy Sabey, Mike and Emma Patterson, Jack and Mary McCann, and Tom and Camilla Tilford.

The University Ministry and VP Mission staff deserve special recognition: Jan O'Brien, Director of Ignatian Programs, Dr. John Freeh, Director of University Ministry, Frs. Jim Meehan, S.J., Matt Gamber, S.J., Leo McKernan and John Rock, S.J., Cherie Peacock, Rev. John Dotson, and of course, Andy van Pelt, AnnMarie Watson, Lisa Meyer, and Florence Robins.

Thanks to Mrs. Betty Wheeler for her special financial contributions to the mission office, to the Magis Institute, and to the Jesuit Community at Gonzaga, which has generously contributed to new ministry programming. It is important to recognize those Jesuits who helped define the new retreat programs by their constant support and active participation, especially, Frs. Kevin Waters, S.J., Mike Connolly, S.J., Jim McDonough, S.J., and John Mossi, S.J.

On the design side, thanks to Mac McCandless who helped so much in shepherding the development of the beautifully renovated University Chapel.

Faculty and colleagues by their own faith and friendship helped enormously to open the campus community to the new programs, including Drs. Dennis Horn, Mary McFarland, Deborah McDonald, Shann Ferch, Max Capobianchi, Bud Barnes, John Hofland, David DeWolf, Paul Buller, Walter Teets, Scott Bozman, Hugh Lefcort, Larry Weiser, LTC Rusty Pritchard and all the ROTC faculty, and Frs. Darrin Connall, Patrick Hartin, and Robert Araujo, S.J.

The University Cabinet always helped with advice and support, especially Harry Sladich, Margot Stanfield, Chuck Murphy, Sue Weitz, Stephen Freedman, Mike Casey, Thayne McCulloh, and of course, Fr. Bob Spitzer, S.J.

And finally, thanks to those students of Gonzaga who responded so generously to God's call as leaders and participants in all the programs. May God allow you to know the gift of grace your efforts have made possible for the greater Gonzaga community.

With Gratitude,

Fr. Bill Watson, S.J.
April 25, 2005

Foreword

Crisp, effective, and captivating communication is a refined art form, whether expressed in concise printed format or crafted for oral delivery from the pulpit. Fr. William Watson, S.J., who lovingly served as Vice President for Mission at Gonzaga University from 1999 to 2004, is truly a master craftsman of word and homily.

The articles and sermons contained in *Reflections and Homilies: The Gonzaga Connection* serve as a lens into the Ignatian tested spirituality of a Jesuit educator and pastoral leader who mystically encounters God in daily events.

His prophetically challenging and thought provoking reflections assist us to examine ordinary events and experiences on deeper levels, spiritually, morally, always with an eye toward enacting justice.

Through his creative and compelling pen, Fr. Watson helps our hearts and minds move in vertical and horizontal directions. With such a meditative eagerness, experience the full impact of the stories and images contained in these pages. Be prepared to enter a personal retreat where you will ponder your relationship with God and encounter the many faces and voices of Jesus found in the marketplace.

Fr. John P. Mossi, S.J.
Director of Ignatian Programs
Gonzaga University

Reflections and Homilies: The Gonzaga Connection
by William M. Watson, S.J.

Table of Contents

Part One

"For The Spirit" columns that appeared in *GONZAGA*, A Quarterly Publication of Gonzaga University

Part Two

Homilies Delivered at Gonzaga University

Part One

"For The Spirit" columns that appeared in *GONZAGA*

A Quarterly Publication of Gonzaga University

The Power of Forgiveness

Summer 2002
GONZAGA

Twenty years ago, a Jesuit told me about his anger toward his mom and dad for the way they treated him when he was growing up. Several weeks after our conversation, I discovered that both his mom and dad had been dead for 15 years. I remember being amazed at how anger and frustration characterized this man's identity even though the people he was angry with were long gone. I never discovered the reasons for his anger and whether they were justified, but I was impressed at the time at how important Christian forgiveness is for us to move on with life in peace and hope.

As a priest I hear many things done to people by others that rightly justify anger – things that are hard simply to "forgive and forget." Many people can't get to the point of forgiveness because they think that forgiving is tantamount to justifying the actions committed against them. However, forgiveness does not excuse injustice. We need to distinguish between the *righteousness* of the anger we feel for genuine injustice, and the Christian call to pray for the grace to forgive those who "have trespassed against us." If we don't forgive others, we run the risk of drowning in our angers and hurts and the cycle of violence and pain never ends – like my friend described above whose energy for living was suffocated by anger over events long-passed.

We live in times of great global and cultural stress. Many of the acts of war and terror in our world are rooted in injustice, both real and perceived. One of the most important things each of us can do to act positively in the face of so many global problems is to search our hearts and see if there is someone or some group God is calling us to forgive. Many individual hearts and souls, healed by the grace of forgiveness, can change the course of history.

God's Mercy

Fall 2002
GONZAGA

Many years ago my dad told me a story about driving home from work. It was a route he had traveled for years without variation. One winter evening, he was stopped at a red light. The light turned green but, for some reason, he did not step on the accelerator. That instant, a tractor-trailer rig ran the red light in the opposite direction. Had my dad done what he "always" did at that stop light, he most likely would have been seriously injured or killed.

I often relate this story to people who wonder why God allows bad things to happen to the world or to them personally. It is very clear to me that the hand of God stopped my dad from taking off at that green light. It makes me wonder how many other times God protected him at potentially disastrous or life-threatening moments. Hundreds? Thousands?

Who can guess how many times the compassionate hand of God intervenes in each of our lives to prevent either some calamity outside of our control or terrible consequences resulting from a bad choice or decision we make ourselves?

We are tethered to God by a covenant of love working directly and through the hearts and hands of many others. He promised to be with us always. As much as we might suffer or witness suffering in the world, one day, when we will no longer look through a glass darkly, we will be amazed to fully comprehend how much love surrounded and protected each and every person all throughout history.

Then we will no longer ask, "Why did you allow this or that to happen?" We will fall on our knees and weep for joy at God's gentle love and compassionate mercy.

Sounds of Silence

Spring 2003
GONZAGA

I have grown accustomed to a single refrain that I have heard now for some 17 years: "Oh Father, I could never be silent for five days. I am just a talkative person. Ask my friends."

This phrase is the common response I receive when I ask people to consider making a five-day retreat. The person's age or professional standing and accomplishments don't seem to matter. Without fail, the response is offered with a wink, a smile and a shrug of the shoulders.

My pastoral instincts have led me to the conclusion that behind the phrase lurks a level of anxiety about silence that ranges from mild discomfort to sheer terror. I know the feeling myself. Every year when I make my own eight-day Ignatian Retreat, I experience a similar fear that stems from having lost touch with my heart to greater or lesser degrees. I don't know what I will discover about myself, my life, my habits, my ambitions, decisions that I have been putting off, changes I need to make, and the simple fear of facing the disappointments, wounds, and personal sinfulness that comes pre-packaged with the human condition.

So how do I market a retreat that sends shockwaves of anxiety through people? It is easy. I have years of testimonies from these retreatants who entered the silence with fears and anxieties and who left the retreat considering it the most powerful experience of their lives. I have heard a different phrase for the same 17 years that goes like this: I can't imagine what I was afraid of in the silence. My biggest anxiety is going back into the 'talking world' for fear that I will lose touch with all the peace I have experienced!"

Gonzaga offers the five-day Ignatian Retreat three times a year. Give yourself the biggest favor of your life and do one. You too will consider it one of the best things you have ever done: that I guarantee.

A Second Chance

Summer 2003
GONZAGA

Life is all about relationships. I know that there are many times in my life where I wish I could have gone back and done something differently to keep an important relationship on track or to repair one that had derailed. Second chances are possible in these situations by simply saying “I am sorry” or “please forgive my stupidity.” Sometimes, however, we don’t have the second chance. What about those times when I needed to say “I love you” or “please forgive me” but death intervened and I lost my last chance? These are the critical missed opportunities to bring closure to important relationships that can cause heartache and loss. But God provides opportunities, even after death, to help us heal these relationships.

I recently spoke with a friend who described how bad blood after a family fight at the age of 16 made him run out on his dad. Later that night, while on duty as a street cop, his dad was shot and killed by a motorist he had stopped to question. My friend lived with his loss for years, wishing that he could have had a second chance to change the last frame of the story. Many years passed and the boy become a man. Financially successful and in excellent health, he was running a full marathon to celebrate his 40th birthday. A few miles short of the goal, he felt chest pain and knew something was terribly wrong. He was having a heart attack and collapsed. Right before he fell, he caught the eye of a policeman in uniform standing at race-side. The officer rushed to him and got him to the hospital in time to save his life.

Gary knew that God had arranged that cop to be there to save his life. He also had no doubt in his heart that the officer was a sign from his dad after all these years that he could let go of the pain he had carried from that evening so long ago. God’s grace provided the second chance he needed to express his love and gratitude to his dad whom he knew was watching over him.

One thing our Christian faith makes clear is that our God is a God of second chances. Death itself cannot prevent God from giving each one of us the opportunities we need to find peace of heart in the important relationships in our lives. Never hesitate to say “I love you” or “I am sorry” when you have the chance. And when those second chances seem lost forever, look for God out of the corner of your eye and God will provide a way.

Coming Home

Fall 2003
GONZAGA

I had dinner recently with a friend 10 years out of college. What occasioned the dinner was his invitation for me to celebrate Mass for his upcoming wedding in January of 2004. In the time since graduation, he has become a successful lawyer here in the Northwest and has many professional accomplishments for which he should be quite proud. Not having seen each other in six years, we enjoyed catching up on our various adventures.

While he shared some of his professional accomplishments over the course of the evening, what dominated his reflections were how much his life was changing as he approached his marriage. He spoke with great fondness of people he was inviting – many college friends with whom he had shared retreat experiences or who had been former roommates. He reflected about growing up on a cattle ranch and the values he learned by being so closely connected to the land and his family.

His older brother, a vice president of a bank in London, would be coming to the wedding but was thinking of retiring soon to become a football coach in rural Montana. His sisters, who had moved away from home and had many accomplishments of their own, were thinking of moving back close to friends and family. His other brother and sister in-law were pregnant but a test revealing a crippling disease the child had inherited would most likely claim his life six weeks after birth.

The funeral for his young nephew, he said, would be close to the time of the wedding and he knew this would be an emotional backdrop for many. The hope he shared was that the support of family would help ease the grief already present. He also talked about how he used to work until 8 or 9 in the evening but how he now promptly left the office at 5:30 to spend time with his fiancee. What struck me so deeply throughout all the conversation was how blessed he felt, even in the face of life's pains and setbacks, and how important it was for him to anchor his future hopes in friends, family, home, and faith.

We all long for a home and we all long to come home. It means different things to each of us but our hearts are set free by relationships – with family, friends and God – and the "hope" of being "home" is connected to all of these. As the time of Thanksgiving and Christmas approach, let us remember the values that humanize our lives. Let's take time to spend with friends and family. Let us be grateful for all that we have received. Let's pray for those who are suffering. And, wherever you are, think of what it means for you to come home. Listen for the hope it offers and consider the choices you might be invited to make to accept the invitation to come home.

Watch It, That Stranger in the Night Could Be Christ

Winter 2004
GONZAGA

Coming home from dinner at my folks' house a few weeks ago, I had nothing else on my schedule for the night. Coming off a busy week and anticipating an even busier one ahead, I was tired and looking forward to collapsing on the couch at home and watching a movie. So I stopped at the local video store on the way home to find something entertaining but not too mentally taxing. It was not a pretty evening. The weather had just turned cold and the night was dark, damp and dreary. Not the kind of night to be out but a great evening for a warm house and a movie.

Coming out of the video store, I made a beeline for the car. From the dark of the night I could see someone out of my peripheral vision approaching. Instinctively, I knew it was a homeless person. I really did not want to be bothered that evening and I tried to quickly unlock my door to escape the encounter.

Too late.

He had a tortured, pockmarked face and a deeply haunted look in his eyes. Not wanting a conversation, I pulled all the change out of my pocket and gave it to him.

"Here," I said, "it is all the change I have." As I started to get into the car, I had a pang of guilt. All I wanted to do was get home and watch a movie in my warm little house on campus. I knew he would walk the streets for the rest of the evening. I stopped and turned around. "What is your first name," I said. He replied, "Anthony."

"Anthony," I said, "I will say a prayer that God watch over you tonight." The haunted look dissolved, his face warmed and he turned and walked away.

As I got into the car and closed the door, I knew I had encountered Christ. No longer did the movie or the warm house seem that important. On the way home, I prayed to God that He would watch over Anthony and everyone walking the streets that night.

Let Us Pray That Life's Complexities Lead Us Toward Justice, Faith

Spring 2004
GONZAGA

Father Mike is a Jesuit classmate of mine and a Naval Reserve chaplain. Last year, about this time, he received orders he was to report for active duty in Iraq. He described to me not only his own fear (he had never been in active combat) but also the inner turmoil he felt as a priest because of Pope John Paul II's statements against the war and his duty to report for deployment. He chose to report for duty I believe not because he supported the war, but because he did not want young soldiers preparing to offer the ultimate sacrifice of their lives to lack spiritual guidance and the sacraments in their hour of greatest need.

I was reminded of Fr. Mike when I received a letter a few months ago from a GU grad and former AGAPE retreat leader stationed in Iraq. First Lt. James Person of the 173rd Airborne Brigade said this:

"Dear Fr. Bill – It seems like ages ago since I've been at Gonzaga but your letter reminds me that graduates have such a focused, idealistic feeling of mission and purpose when they leave Gonzaga. Without reflection and prayer, it is easy to lose that focus... Before I was deployed to Iraq I prayed that my participation would serve a higher purpose. I want to start an "adopt a school" (program) between American and Iraqi schools. I have a list of about 800 here in Kirkuk alone."

Fr. Mike prayed over his troops a week after Ash Wednesday on the eve the war. At the end of the official conflict, not one solider under his command had been injured or killed. James' program is taking flight, as Gonzaga and James' family in Montana have helped him get word out about his work as a citizen-solider.

Life oftentimes presents us with difficult choices and we may be forced to engage in adventures that we can't fully support. We can choose to participate, however, because we hope to prevent a greater evil and hope to promote a greater good.

As we emerge from the season of Lent and Easter, let us remember the sacrifices of those many people who placed themselves in harm's way to help each one of us in our lives. Let us also pray that our choices to engage in the moral complexities of these most challenging times would, by our faith in God, help prevent evil and promote God's kingdom of justice and peace.

A Different Story of Jesus and Peter

Summer 2004
GONZAGA

There is a Jesuit school program in Colombia called "Faith and Joy." The program educates children who fall through the cracks of Colombian civil society. Visiting one of the sites in Medellín last August, I met an 11 year-old by the name of Peter.

The harsh and cruel situations he had faced in his short life were not evident in the radiant smile on his face. Born to a single mother, he was cast out on the street at a young age when his mom met a new boyfriend who conditioned the relationship on Peter's departure.

Living on the streets of Medellín, he found occasional friendship in an aged grandmother. He then contracted terminal cancer and was given six months to live.

When I met Peter, he had recently been given a clean bill of health by a doctor who had no medical explanation for Peter's complete and total remission of the cancer.

Peter introduced himself to me by saying; "Jesus loves me, he healed me!"

The conviction with which he spoke indicated to me that he personally knew Jesus and that Jesus not only conveyed to Peter his deep love for him but that it was that love which healed Peter.

Peter's story tells us that the sometimes harsh and cruel situations of life have an answer in Jesus' personal love of us.

The God who does not take his eye off the sparrow holds each of us lovingly in the heart of his Son.

Perhaps each of us can learn from Peter and take the risk of inviting God into our lives. The God of love wants to give each one of us hope and healing and a radiant smile that only love can convey.

We Are Called to Hope, No Matter Our Struggles

Fall 2004
GONZAGA

Several people close to me have been diagnosed with cancer. Many other friends have relatives or loved ones who also have been diagnosed. Quite a few people in both groups seem to me to be too young to be facing such potentially life-threatening consequences.

A friend of mine, Brian McDermott, S.J., rector of the Georgetown Jesuit Community, gave a homily at a Mass I attended in June. His reflections were on three men in the community who had just recently passed on, one very unexpectedly.

He said that all his life he had believed that our efforts as human beings and as Christians should be focused on this present world to make it a better place, and not the world to come. By focusing on the world to come, he said, we risked not attending to the important mission God is giving us. However in light of growing older, and reflecting on three men whom he had just laid to rest, he was having second thoughts.

He said that these men had always belonged to God and the ultimate purpose of their lives was to be with God forever – that they now they had completed their mission for which this life was simply a preparation.

I remembered this homily as I heard news of my friends' diagnoses and was reminded as well of my own mortality. The New Testament reminds us: "No eye has seen, no ear has heard, no mind has conceived what God has prepared for those who love him."

We are called to the hope and belief that no matter what life throws at us, even life-threatening illness, that God has a plan of eternal joy. Our limited capacity to see the plan can create frustration, fear or even the belief that God has abandoned us. But each one of us has been born from love and will return to the Love from which we were given birth.

Let us remember those who are sick and suffering that they can know God's peace and hope. And knowing the Love to which each of us is called, let this ultimate mission of life shape each morning, encounter, and decision as we prepare to see what God has ready for those who love him.

Part Two

Homilies Delivered at Gonzaga University

Stand Firm in Faith

Mass of the Holy Spirit
Gonzaga University
September 15, 1999
Feast of Our Lady of Sorrows
Readings: Joel 3:1-5; Rm 12 1-8; Lk 9 18-27

At the beginning of each academic year, Catholic colleges and universities offer a Mass of the Holy Spirit. At the commencement of this academic year on the threshold of the Third Millennium of Christianity, let us explore together what this event can mean for us personally as Catholics, Christians or members of other faith communities. What can it mean for us as an academic community open to the inspirations of faith? Let us also look at what this Sacrificial celebration and invocation of the Spirit – in this *academic setting* – can mean for our part in the renewal of culture.

So let me begin with a story – a true story….

The first chapter of his biography begins like a Tom Clancy spy novel. There is even a Jack Ryan character. He writes: “I knew when I dialed the U.S. State Department that I would reach my party immediately. “Yes?” It was Jack Scanlan, Deputy Assistant Secretary for Eastern Europe, and exactly the person I wanted to speak to.

“Jack, it’s Romek”… I hesitated, then let it spill out all at once. “I’m asking for protection, Jack; I want the president to grant me and my family political asylum.”

The person writing is Francis Romuld Spasowski. At the time of this phone call in 1981, Spasowski is Poland’s ambassador to the U.S. and its most senior post-war diplomat. This simple phone call also is transforming Spasowski into the highest-ranking Communist official ever to defect to the West.

After hanging up the phone, dozens of FBI and Washington D.C. police cars block the streets leading to the Polish ambassador’s house in Washington. Romek and his wife Wanda and their daughter Misha hurriedly collect a few personal items. The Polish crystal candlesticks on the altar today are two family heirlooms they manage to pack in their rush to escape. The Soviet KGB will soon know of their planned escape and try to block them from leaving the extra-territorial property of the ambassador's residence. They have to hurry. They will face certain death in Poland if they are captured and deported. The long arm of the Soviet government will force the premier, General Jaruzelski, to deal severely with Spasowski and his family to stem the political damage from this humiliating defection, especially in light of the deepening crisis raging in Poland over the Solidarity trade union.

"After hanging up the phone, the past forty years of Spasowski's life rush past him. He feels a great weight falling from him as he suddenly realizes he is free of the clutches of the Polish secret police, their constant shadowings, insinuations, Byzantine parlor games, their obscene lies to implement martial law to crush Solidarity. Forty years of life so tautly woven into People's Poland, is spinning off with them. It had taken him forty years to come to this, and only when he put down the receiver, did he see his decision in its naked reality."

Several days after the Spasowskis escaped and were rescued by the U.S. government, they met privately with President Reagan. It is late December of 1981, just before Christmas. Reagan's Christmas message to the American people a few days later is dedicated almost exclusively to the events in Poland. At Spasowski's request, Reagan asks Americans to put candles in their windows at Christmas as a sign of their solidarity with the suffering people of Poland, and Lech Walesa, the leader of the Solidarity trade union who has just been imprisoned. On November 9, 1989, just eight years later, the Berlin Wall will be pulled down.

In the last year of his life, I was Romek's personal priest as he lay dying of bone cancer in his apartment in Northern Virginia. I was also honored to preach at his funeral at the National Shrine of the Immaculate Conception in Washington, D.C. Prior to becoming a Christian, he had been a convinced atheist most his adult life and a committed communist since age 16. Of the many stories he told me about his life leading up to his defection, I asked him if there was one event that gave him the inner strength to make the phone call. He said it was the Pope's first visit to Poland in the spring of 1980.

Romek was in Warsaw for John Paul's visit. It was an anniversary of sorts for Spasowski. It was forty years ago in Warsaw that Romek last saw his father Wladyslaw. Tears in his eyes, 19-year-old Romek embraces his father as the cyanide capsule went to work. He promised his father that he would carry on his work for the communist cause. Wladyslaw Spasowski was at this time Poland's leading communist intellectual and author of the famous manifesto: *Liberation of Man.* He committed suicide in Warsaw's botanical garden to escape the Nazis after the Russian government denied political asylum to him and his son. Romek carried the cause for the next 40 years.

But today would be a new day. Because his travel to Warsaw was last-minute, Romek told me he could not get a pass for the Mass in Victory Square. From four blocks away, straining to hear the Pope's homily, he was riveted by every word. Chills were going down his spine, he told me, half from fear and half from excitement. The loudspeakers were echoing: "One cannot understand himself without Christ," the pope said. "One cannot understand the history of the Polish nation or this City of Warsaw which would be abandoned by its allies in an unequal battle that would leave it in rubble. Christ too lay beneath that rubble!"

Romek cried when his father died. Forty years later, he was again in Warsaw crying, not tears of grief, but of hope. Standing alone by a street light, unable see the pope, barely able to hear the last of John Paul's homily, he said, seemed to echo from a great depth, and engrave itself on his memory: "May Your Spirit descend on us! May Your Spirit descend on us! And renew the face of the earth. This earth! Amen!"

Romek Spasowski fought for the liberation of humankind by means of the socialist principles learned at his father's knee. The biography I have quoted from is called the *Liberation of One* – a direct counterpoint to his father's famous communist manifesto, *The Liberation of Man.* Romek personally discovered that full human liberation comes from another source – The Spirit, working in individual human hearts, not ideologies enforced by the state. The Polish people gathered in Victory Square in June of 1981 were challenged not to be afraid but to believe that their greatest cultural achievements of the last 1,000 years were directly connected to their faith. They would finally stand united, firm in faith, against the threats of Jaruzelski's puppet government controlled by Moscow.

For the past 20 years, John Paul II has been traveling the world bringing the message that Christianity is not a threat to culture but its catalyst, its way to fullness. In his 1990 Apostolic Constitution, he pleas for the culture of the Catholic university to be fully open to the Spirit. A Mass of the Holy Spirit then, is a momentous event. Far from being an empty ritual, it is a call to each of us – student, faculty or staff, administrator and board member – to stand open to the power of the Spirit, to live in the freedom of the Spirit as the ground of our identity, individual and corporate.

As individuals and as a university community, we want to accomplish great things. This is a noble aspiration firmly grounded in what Ignatius taught his followers. It is called the "greater good." We remember that our Ignatian heritage calls us not just to the good Gonzaga is capable of accomplishing, but *the greater good; one common good.* And for a Catholic-Jesuit institution that *greater common good* is a living faith that gives birth to justice.

A living, energetic, dynamic faith is the spark that is needed to make our educational structures serve justice. The 1974 Congregation of the Society of Jesus put it most succinctly with the words of Ignatius when they wrote that in carrying out the mission of justice, we should be convinced, today, more than ever, that "the means which unite the human instrument with God and so dispose it to be wielded dexterously by His divine hand, are more effective than those which equip it in relation to other people." In other words, to add a new phrase to the bumper sticker "If you want Peace, work for Justice": "If you want Peace and Justice help people open themselves to the power of God's Spirit working in their lives." Nothing new here. Jesus said it better in the Gospel: "Love the Lord your God with all your heart, all your mind and all your strength. And your neighbor as yourself." Jesus wants us to be captured by Love in a relationship that transforms affect, intellect and will, so that gospel justice can flourish on this earth.

And even with the collapse of Eastern totalitarianism, we still have a long way to go. Anyone with eyes to see knows that injustice is not limited to the former Eastern Block countries. In many respects, the challenges we face to transform our American culture are just as formidable as those faced by Spasowski and the Polish people who stood in Victory Square in June of 1981. Our Catholic university culture is as tautly woven into the American culture as Spasowski's life was into the People's Poland. In fact, it might even be more difficult for us Westerners to see the challenges we face because of our freedoms.

A Jesuit friend's mother, who spent time in a Nazi concentration camp, told her children as they were growing up that she felt sorry for them. Even with all the suffering she endured, she had it easier then her children. In her world, she could tell the difference between good and evil. For them, living in America at the end of this century, it was impossible to discern clearly right from wrong. Truth no longer seems to exist.

The loss of a sense of truth is a manifestation of a culture untethered from faith. For many of our contemporaries, as the Jesuits in their 1974 General Congregation wrote, are "dazzled and even dominated by the achievements of the human mind, forgetting or rejecting the mystery of the man's ultimate meaning, have thus lost the sense of God." And as our century has shown us so well, a loss of a sense of God and ultimate goodness – the common good – inevitably leads to injustice.

Bernard Lonergan in his *Method in Theology*, calls injustice *social corruption* and *decline* and is aware that such decline inflicts cultures with conflicting ideologies that cripple authentic human progress. Decline or injustice begins in the disordered desire for pure material gain and power but soon leaches into the mass media the "stylish journals, literary movements, the educational process, and the reigning philosophies." Like John Paul II and the Jesuits in 1974, Lonergan knows that fundamental liberation results from neither coercion, propaganda nor intellectual argument, but from religious faith. It is religious faith that liberates human reasonableness from ideological prisons, says Lonergan. For only the Spirit can bring unity in the face of conflicting ideologies and the kinds of injustice and decline that pervert human cultures.

The Jesuit university must, as the 1995 General Congregation insisted, have Jesuits and others committed to the search "for the fullness of truth." The Congregation's fathers assure us that "despite occasional appearances to the contrary, the truth we seek will ultimately be one. That truth, rooted as it is in God, will make us free." (GC 34 # 415)

Openness to the spirit will bring each of us to a new level of faith, truth, freedom, and peace. But a willing embrace of the freedom the Spirit of God offers is something we cannot take for granted. As Dostoyevsky reminds us, when given the choice between freedom and bread i.e., between authentic human living and the comfort of what we know, people all too often choose the bread of comfort. And to further complicate the situation, Christ reminds us in today's Gospel that when we *do* follow him – He who is Way, Truth, and Life – we may also encounter the resistance of the world.

But we are challenged anew today not to fear living under the Spirit of God. We are promised that it is the way to freedom and eternal life. In their openness to that calling down of the Spirit, the people of Poland were transformed individually and as a people. Solidarity ultimately triumphed and culture was transformed.

Thomas Cahill, in the final pages of his book, *How the Irish Saved Civilization*, surveys our modern culture and sees in it many of the characteristic traits that led the Roman Empire to collapse so swiftly some 1,500 years ago. The percentage of underclass in the world increases daily. The gap between rich and poor has never been wider. And the cultures of the developed world become more socially fragmented and filled with ennui even as wealth piles up.

But in times of great cultural stress, the most desperate of times, the gifts of the Spirit will be more abundant than ever, the reading from Joel reminds us.

Cahill, too, is hopeful. He says that the world always seems to be divided into Romans and Catholics. The Romans are the ones who believe in technology, wealth and/or power as the way to salvation. And the Catholics, with a small "c," the universalists, are the ones who, seeking first the Kingdom, put faith in God not things. It is these alone who can see the face of God in all people. If our civilization is to be saved, he says, it will happen because of Romans, not saints.

This means that saving hope for the future may not be germinating in the boardrooms of Silicon Valley, Wall Street or London, but in a house for the dying in a back street of Calcutta begun by an Albanian peasant nun. It can also mean that the brightest future of higher education, Catholic or other, i.e. education that positively advances human culture and Gospel values, may not be at Stanford, MIT, or Cambridge England, but in small colleges like Gonzaga that are open to faith for a new direction and mission. We mustn't forget we are named after a young Italian, Aloysius Gonzaga, who himself, *for love of Christ*, gave up vast wealth and power to serve the dying poor in the streets of Rome.

Romuld Spasowski ends his biography this way: "The greatest day of my life came on April 9, 1985, when I was received into the Church at the age of sixty-four. As I was baptized...I asked myself whether I deserved the grace of forgiveness and reconciliation with Him who liberated man's greatest hope. In joining myself to Christ, I felt at last one with Poland's martyred people."

Let each of us today join ourselves to the Spirit of God so that our individual lives and our corporate efforts give birth to a faith that can bring hope, peace and justice to the suffering of *our* world. The promise is indeed great. There is a role for each of us to play, no matter our Christian background or faith tradition, for there are many gifts animated by the One Spirit of God to serve this one common good. It is a choice we each need to make. Faith is a relationship of love. Love cannot be mandated. At the crucifixion, the Father forever turns away from coercion as a strategy to bring peace. Love can only be freely accepted and offered. And through a miracle of grace Christ today again freely give us himself. His Sacrifice of Redemptive Love is made truly present to us in this Eucharist so we are strengthened for the journey.

Let us therefore, choose to live our lives, individually and corporately under the power of the Spirit of God. Let us say yes to the invitation of Love and bind ourselves today to the Spirit of God as servants of Christ's mission. As a sign of our *solidarity* on this mission, let us together pray to the Holy Spirit with the prayer printed in our program:

Come Holy Spirit, Renew the Hearts of your Faithful
Enkindle within us the Fire of Divine Love
Send Forth your Spirit and we shall be recreated
And you will renew the face of the earth.

"May Your Spirit descend on us! May Your Spirit descend on us! And renew the face of the earth."

This earth! Amen!

Relationships: Build One With God and You Will Find Peace

Baccalaureate Homily
Gonzaga University
May 12, 2001
St. Aloysius Church

I. Commencement

Think back to your days in high school and your graduation. What do you most remember? At the center of events both joyful and sad, maybe even painful, I am sure are the relationships, more than anything else, that you remember the most.

Think back to your own GEL weekend or your first visit to Gonzaga. What were you looking for? Yes, you were interested in classes and academic programs, extracurricular activities, and opportunities to get involved and to serve. But more than anything you probably remember that people were kind and friendly and that you could *imagine* Gonzaga being a *HOME* for yourself.

Remember your move-in day and those first fun and anxious weeks of school? What were you most concerned about? Probably something like; "Will I make friends here at Gonzaga?"

Try to remember a time when you may have consumed a little too much of that carbonated beverage brewed from hops. Can you remember? Can you remember? I am sure that some of those times were because you were with the great friends you always hoped you would have at Gonzaga. I am also certain that some of the times might have been because of friendships lost or relationships broken.

And try to remember that one spiritual experience that changed everything. Did it have to do with knowing yourself as being loved and cherished? Did it open your life to a hope you had only dreamed about? Did you find the forgiveness you never thought was possible? Did you feel connected with God's creation and the beautiful people he created? Most probably, yes to all of these!

Commencement is about new beginnings and its poignancy comes not only from the hope of the future but of the bittersweet partings that have to happen when we move on to new things in life. Leave takings, and commencements are sacred times. They connect us powerfully to what is most elemental in human experience and remind us who we are, where we are from, and where we are going in the future. Life is always a series of beginnings and endings, endings and beginnings.

The hope at times of commencement is rooted in the expectation that the best is yet to come – both in terms of friendships and opportunities. The sadness comes from having to say goodbye to friends and the unconscious anxiety about the fragility and lack of permanency of our relationships that shadows us all our lives.

Tomorrow is Mothers Day. Mothers know probably more than anyone else the mystery of life's beginnings and its inevitable separations. For mothers are connected to the mystery of life in a most unique way.

I recently visited friends whose marriage ceremony I presided at and whose two young children I baptized. We were getting ready to go out to dinner. The baby sitter had arrived and as we started to go out the door, young 18 month old Michael was running from room to room trying to find mommy. Tears were streaming down his face and his crying was the kind that expresses a deep fear. He was being separated from the security of his mom.

Mom's temptation can be to hold him and bring him comfort – but she knew that he would not grow if she held him. For authentic love has to both hold on and let go. Mature love knows the right time for both holding and letting go. Mothers have a unique knowledge that we are never really fully at peace in this world, and thus never fully at home either. It is the image of Michael running from room to room trying to find that security and comfort that symbolizes the endings and beginnings of our human lives. We are pulled forward always, searching for that ultimate comfort and peace, relationship that will last, and love that will never end.

II. The Significance of Today's Gospel

Today's Gospel is the archetypal *leave taking and commencement* in one single story. This section of John's Gospel which details Jesus' last meal with his friends begins this way: "Now before the Feast of Passover when Jesus knew that his hour had come to depart out of this world...."

Jesus takes leave of his disciples, yet this separation, surely marked by confusion and sadness on the part of his friends, is a leave taking and a commencement unlike any other. For it is a leave taking and a commencement that forever changes the world. It is the *first* leave taking in human history that promises not the *separation* from friendship, love, and hope but *Loves Ultimate Fulfillment.* "Do not be distressed or fearful – I go away for a while yet I come back to you."

Jesus' commencement will lead him to his life's work – the Sacrifice of Love that will bring about the end of death and open up the way to love that will never end – friendship that will last forever. Jesus sends his disciples and followers the *Spirit* who will lead us to see the way to all truth. He Promises ***HIS Peace*** – a peace that the world cannot give – as both a *Gift* and a *Farewell Blessing.*

And Jesus tells his disciples all that is about to happen so that they will *Believe in Him – Believe in Him as the one who has come to bring life, love, forgiveness, and open the way to the eternity of love that our hearts have been made to desire.*

The Eucharist we share today is the fruit of Jesus' labor. It is the Sacrificial Meal of Love, the great AGAPE Feast, that promises us that we will be forever united with each other *in Him* - And, it promises us that one day our leave takings will cease and we will share, in love and friendship, an eternal banquet in the Kingdom to come.

III. What do we do in the meantime?

So how do we live our lives as we leave Gonzaga? We are told by Jesus not to be sad, distressed or fearful, yet we *always* fall into this trap. How can we find the *peace* the world cannot give? How can we *believe* in Him?

I would like to take you back to the first week of your freshman year in order to find the practical advice on living in this message of hope as we leave Gonzaga. On the Friday of your first week of class, September 5, 1997, Mother Teresa of Calcutta, the Saint of the Gutters, died. I think this remarkable woman whose entrance into the Kingdom coincided with the first weekend of your college careers can give us some advice on how to live our lives in both the peace and belief that Jesus calls us to share.

The Peace the World Cannot Give

On February 3, 1994 at the National Prayer Breakfast in Washington, D.C., Mother Teresa said the following: "Let us thank God for the opportunity he has given us today to have come here to pray together. We have come here especially to pray for peace, joy and love. We are reminded that Jesus came to bring the good news to the poor. He told us what is that good news is when he said: "My peace I leave with you. My peace I give to you." He came not to give the peace of the world, which is only that we don't bother each other. He came to give the peace of heart which comes from loving – from doing good for others."

I invite you to always love the poor, the unloved, and the unlovely. Set your lives on the course of *doing good* and *being good.* It is in service to others that you will find the peace the world cannot give. Use all your gifts and talents in service of a mission of love. When you are sad, distressed, or fearful, find someone who is more sad, distressed and fearful that yourself and serve them. And as Mother Theresa always said, sometimes that service can be as simple as a smile.

Believe In Me

Mother Teresa was passionately in love with the person of Christ. So was St. Ignatius. Both excelled at putting love into action – in showing that love is expressed more in deeds than words. But both also were passionately in love with the person of Christ and were not afraid to express that love to the world.

One of Mother Teresa's most famous prayers is this:

"If we pray, we will believe, if we believe we will love, if we love we will serve."

Take time each day to get to know Christ better. There is no more productive way you can spend your time. He will bring comfort and hope, he will bring healing and forgiveness, he will help you get through any situation that can or will arise in the future. *This is your faith. Take time to be with Christ so you can believe in Him.* There is no better way to spend time productively than to waste time with the Lord. Let me repeat that. There is no more productive way to spend your time than to waste some time each day in prayer with the Lord.

And finally, combine your concern for others, your service, with your faith in Christ Jesus. Gonzaga wants to "educate people the world needs most." In order for that to happen, we all need to let our love of God grow daily, and to live that love *practically* in the world. These are the two poles of the Great Commandment: Love the Lord your God with all your heart, with all your mind, and with all your strength – and love your neighbor as yourself. Both poles of the Great Commandment are combined in this prayer of St. Teresa of Calcutta.

People are often unreasonable, illogical and self-centered;
Forgive them anyway.
If you are kind, people may accuse you of selfish, ulterior motives;
Be kind anyway.
If you are successful, you will win some false friends and some true enemies;
Succeed anyway.
If you are honest and frank, people may cheat you;
Be honest and frank anyway.
What you spend years building, someone could destroy overnight;
Build anyway.
If you find serenity and happiness, they may be jealous;
Be happy anyway.
Give the world your best and it may never be enough;
Give the world your best anyway.
You see, in the final analysis, it is between you and God;
It was never between you and them anyway.

Goodbye. We will miss you. God Speed and come home to Gonzaga often.

Always Trust Your Faith

Ash Wednesday Homily
Gonzaga University
March 5, 2003
St. Aloysius Student 10 p.m. Mass

Every year when I am preparing to write my Ash Wednesday homily, I ask myself one question: This year, do I need to be good cop or bad cop? This year, I decided to be a bad cop.

I have always had good teeth. In fact, I have always been proud of my teeth. They are naturally straight and I have had few cavities. The dentist always told me to brush after meals, floss regularly, and come in twice a year for a checkup. But since I never seemed to have any problems those wise recommendations fell on deaf ears, especially about coming in twice a year for checkups. The way I figured it, he was out to make a buck, and since I did not have any problems, well, it was not going to work with me.

A number of years ago, I went in for a checkup, my first in five years. While the dentist was not pleased with the plaque buildup, he said my teeth looked very good. The pride returned – that "I told you so" feeling washed over me again. A week later when I had to return to go over my x-rays, he sat me down and we went over the results together. In short, $5,000 worth of work was needed, all due to my poor dental hygiene. The dentist pulled out a book with larger-than-life pictures of open mouths with teeth in varying stages of gum disease and other maladies. He looked at me calmly and rather nonchalantly, with no judgment in his voice, said, "Do you want to keep your original teeth?" I was angry and felt manipulated. In hindsight, I knew the anger was due to the fact that I did not want to face the fact that I was at fault. Worse still, I was being confronted with my own pride and the reality that I would have to change some patterns of behavior that were well ingrained after so many years. I was deeply resentful of someone telling me that unless I changed, I would lose my teeth.

If you will pardon the rather crude analogy, the Lenten Season is somewhat like a dental checkup for the soul. While we all would rather have chicken soup for the soul, if we don't get that checkup, we may be forced to eat chicken soup more than we might wish. We might feel pride about our lives and think things are A-OK. *"The way I have lived in the past has suited me just fine, thank you!"* But Jesus, through the Church, calls us every day, and particularly during Lent, to turn from sinful habits that are corrosive to our souls, that erode our happiness, fracture our friendships, threaten our earth, and possibly even rob us of eternal life – things all a little more significant than cavities and gum disease!

We all sin. The prophet Joel (2:12-18) makes that clear when he calls the entire assembly to fast: the bridegroom and bride, the elders, the children, the infant at breast, and the priests and ministers of the Lord. We are to turn back to the Lord with all our hearts. When we turn to the Lord, we can have faith that God won't turn from us because Jesus is the compassion of the Father, who comes to take away our sins. That is what St. Paul means in the second reading (2 Cor. 5:20-6:2) when he calls himself an ambassador for God and tells us to be reconciled to God. St. Paul reminds us that Jesus took on our sins; that He became sin for us so that we could be free.

What are some of the ways we can stray from God? Do these indicate some of the ways our hearts might need to be turned back to God? We can be helped by taking a look at what our tradition, being faithful to the Old and New Covenants and the teachings of Christ, has called sin. If conversion is described as turning our heart back toward God, it might be helpful to consider sin as turning our hearts away, not only from God, but from our own heart, i.e., our truest self. Sin, then, is not some abstract theory, but distorts the very core of our human identity. In going through the New Catechism of the Catholic Church, I wanted to see how it describes the Commandments in modern language and practice. Here is a little of what the Church says about sin in our own day and age:

First Commandment: You shall love the Lord your God and Him alone shall you serve. Sins against this commandment are sins directly against God and Faith. Voluntary doubt refuses to hold as true or disregards what God has revealed and the Church proposes for belief. Incredulity is the neglect of revealed truth or the willful refusal to assent to it. Refusal to hope can be a refusal to believe that God can forgive your sins. We can sin against God's love by indifference to faith, being ungrateful for what God has accomplished for us in creation, and redemption, being spiritually lazy or even holding on to a deep-seated hatred of God. Atheistic humanism rejects or denies the existence of God. This particular sin is very fashionable in academic circles today. Idolatry is divinizing what is not God and placing something that is not God in the center of our life and worshiping it – money, power, pleasure, and the like. Remember Golum in the *Lord of the Rings, The Two Towers* – "IT'S MINE, IT'S MINE. MY PRECIOUS, MY PRECIOUS!" Look what idolatry did to him!!

Second Commandment: The Name of the Lord is Holy. It is sinful to abuse God's Holy Name in any way whatsoever. I remember a Jewish psychology professor at Georgetown complaining to me, a Catholic priest, about the kind of public swearing and profanity that seemed perfectly acceptable on Georgetown's campus.

Third Commandment: The Sabbath is Holy. It is sinful to skip Mass on Sundays and Holy Days unless there is a sound reason that prevents our being able to attend, such as sickness and the like. Exams, skiing, football, basketball, golf, and dining out are *not* sound reasons. It is sinful because we cut ourselves off from the life of sanctifying grace that we need to live our Christian life. It is a serious violation of the holiness of the Eucharist to receive Communion if we have missed Mass willfully on Sunday or Holy Days (or committed any other grave sin).

Fourth Commandment: Honor your Father and Mother. Our parents are more important than any other people on the face of the earth in relation to those whom we owe respect and honor. We are to give proper respect and honor to our parents, even though their own love might be imperfect. We have a greater responsibility to love them than other people. Do I forgive them when I need to and thank them for the gift of life they have given to me?

Fifth Commandment: Do not kill. Of course, intentional homicide is wrong. This is a no-brainer! Direct abortion, which is abortion willed as an end or a means, bears the penalty of excommunication for those who do it or assist others in doing it. This is pretty significant. We are to have a proper dignity of our person, so it is wrong to give in to a cult of the body or to eat, drink, smoke tobacco, or take medicines in excess. Scandal is an attitude or behavior that leads another person to do something evil and hence, is sinful, even if the act committed is done not by us, but by someone else. Scandal is sinful because it leads to the death of someone else's spiritual life.

Sixth Commandment: Do not commit adultery. Being faithful to the Gospels, the Church teaches that all sexual relationships outside the covenant of marriage are sinful, even if the relationship in which the sex takes place is a loving and caring one. If a person has so acted, he or she should seek sacramental reconciliation before receiving Communion.

Seventh Commandment: Do not steal. Stealing or destroying someone else's property is sinful. Stealing someone else's intellectual property, such as copying papers or cheating on exams, is sinful. Breaking contracts that are morally just is sinful. We are to respect the integrity of God's creation. Animals, plants, and other natural resources are destined for the common good of all humanity, and to abuse them or waste them is sinful.

Eighth Commandment: This is another much overlooked commandment. Do not bear false witness against your neighbor. Misrepresenting the truth in relation to others is sinful. As Christians, we are called to bear witness in public to the truth of our Faith so to follow Jesus' public example. Lying, or twisting the facts to give a distorted perception of reality of another's character, is sinful, whether in the media, print or with spoken words. Our tradition has a big word for it – Calumny – is ruining the good name of another and is sinful. How do we speak about others behind their backs? Adulation of others, which leads them to conduct that is malicious or perverse is sinful as well. Do you egg people on to sinful actions? "Go ahead, have another shot!" This is sinful, even though you did not commit the action you encouraged!

Ninth Commandment: Do not covet your neighbor's wife or husband. This commandment has to do with lust of the eyes and flesh, in the heart of our desiring. It speaks to movements of our sensual appetite, which are sinful. So lusting after someone who is not my wife or husband is sinful. In this same vein, eroticism and use of pornography, in whatever form, is sinful, no matter what you read in the student press.

Tenth Commandment: You shall not covet anything that is your neighbor's. This commandment has to do with greed and the desire for the goods of someone else; hence, sins of this sort are situated in our hearts. So it is sinful to have a passion for riches and the power they bring. Likewise, it is sinful to be envious of someone else's wealth. St. Augustine thought envy was *the* diabolical sin. Cain's envy of Abel's sacrifice actually led him to murder his brother. These sins originate in the idolatry prohibited by the first three commandments.

So what might you do for Lent? Jesus, in the Gospel, calls us to do good works, to pray, and to fast. What you do should be designed to help you get at that particular pattern of sinfulness which cuts at the heart of your true identity, and thus robs you of your inherent freedom as a child created in the image of a loving and merciful God. If you prayerfully take stock of your life, you will know what you are to do and how far you are to go with your good works, prayer and fasting. If you need help, ask for spiritual advice from a confessor. Sometimes the best way to counteract a particular vice or sin is to practice positive virtues. So while giving things up can be very helpful to grow in holiness, doing things to counteract our sinful tendencies can also be a great way to "fast" during this great and holy season.

Just remember that as the Church calls us to know our sinfulness because she has a divine mandate to do so, she also has the same mandate to proclaim the Lamb of God who takes away the sins of the world. The great mission of the Church is to make His saving grace available to anyone who seeks it, no matter how lost or broken they might be. Ours is a joyful faith, which will lead us to freedom and peace in this life and eternal life in the Kingdom to come.

So this Lent, brush your teeth, floss, get a checkup and, with God's grace, begin to change those habits that need changing. Be reconciled to God and come home to your true self. Christ, in joy, awaits you.

It's Not What We Have, But Who We Become

Baccalaureate Homily
Gonzaga University
Saturday, May 10, 2003
Martin Centre

Fr. Peter Hans Kolvenbach, S.J., Superior General of the Society of Jesus, recently wrote the following about the mission of Jesuit higher education:

Today's prominent ideology reduces the human world to a global jungle whose primordial law is the survival of the fittest. Students who subscribe to this view want to be equipped with well-honed professional and technical skills in order to compete in the market and secure one of the relatively scarce fulfilling and lucrative jobs available. This is the success which many students (and parents!) expect. All American universities, Jesuit included, are under tremendous pressure to opt entirely for success in this sense. But what our students want – and deserve – includes but transcends this "worldly success" based on marketable skills. ***For the real measure of our Jesuit universities lies in who our students become.***

A Gonzaga education, as Fr. Kolvenbach states, is rooted in a vision of the Gospel of Jesus Christ that looks at everything: every possibility, every tragedy, every opportunity, every country and every person through the eyes of God who is justice and mercy for his people. We see echoes of this truth in the reading from Proverbs that proclaims this God as guarding the paths of justice and protecting the way of his pious ones. We recognize these lofty ideals from Paul's letter to the Philippians that calls us to think of what is true, honorable, just, pure, lovely, gracious and worthy of praise. And we hear the testimony of Christ in John's Gospel urging us to be faithful to his word, the word of the Father, to live our lives in God's love – for faith and justice are undivided in the Gospel which teaches that faith makes its power felt through love.

A time of commencement, especially in the context a Baccalaureate Mass at a Jesuit university, is a time to take stock of how well we have accomplished in our students the mission we proclaim. To reflect on how well we have done, permit me to share with you some reflections I received from students whom I asked to think about blessings, missed opportunities, future anxieties, and ultimate hopes for their lives. While time permits us to share only a sampling of comments, what we hear today is consistent with the spirit of each and every student who wrote.

Nate Macklin

1. Without a doubt, the greatest blessing during my time at Gonzaga was the Florence program. It not only exposed me to some of the greatest Catholic art, culture, and history, but it made me grow up.

2. If I could go back, I probably would have taken better advantage of the incredible volunteer opportunities through CCASL or other programs that work directly with the Spokane community.

3. What concern me are the transitions. I think I am prepared for anything, Gonzaga has taught me a certain level of confidence in my professional, personal and spiritual life; most importantly Gonzaga has instilled in each of us the impossibility of divorcing any of those three from each other, especially the spiritual.

4. My deepest hope is that I return to my 20-year reunion not with an incredible amount of money, nor with a beach house in Palm Springs. Instead, I hope to return and tell myself and my friends that I've successfully found the vocation that truly utilizes my personal, professional and spiritual gifts to their greatest potential.

Melissa Wood

1. The Gonzaga Tennis Team, AGAPE, Summer in Florence 2001, Residence Hall Staff, SEARCH, The Ignatian Retreat, and many, many, many professors, university officials, and other university staff members.

2. Overall, I can't think of anything major that I feel I missed out on.

3. The only concern I have right now is that many of my friends will be leaving Gonzaga and I may never get to see them again. I know that my path will be laid before me as God wants it to be – and I will always cherish those friendships.

4. My deepest hope is that I will be able to continue on with my faith life as I have here at Gonzaga. That is something that I will miss almost immediately after leaving, and will always strive to re-create in my life wherever I may end up.

Chris Tomassi

1. On a fall day in Florence, Fr. Tony Lehmann took me and a small group of students to a Carthusian monastery to show us the lifestyle he had lived for 18 years. Listening to Fr. Tony's wisdom, and taking his advice, I was immediately able to truly grasp how amazing life really is. It was incredible.

2. If I could redo anything during my four years at Gonzaga, it would be to simply get involved in the school earlier.

3. Spiritually, I worry that I may lose some of my faith when I leave Gonzaga because the opportunities to further it here are so numerous.

4. In the end, I will work hard to be kind. Sometimes, just being nice to someone really changes their day. If I could do anything with my life, I would end up in politics, as a U.S. senator with the hope that I could pass laws that would make the world a better place. It's kind of corny, but I truly think that I can make a difference.

Brady Strahl

1. I had the opportunity to spend Easter weekend in Bosnia. Our time in Medjugorje called to mind the importance of faith in a foreign land... Seeing Sarajevo, only years after the war, is among the most humbling experiences...seeing the devastation

of country first hand made me *forever* realize how blessed I am.

2. No real regrets stand out here.

3. Anxieties? Since August of 1999, I have been surrounded by the most caring, compassionate and selfless people. I'm not yet sure where I will be next year but I am comforted knowing that thousands of students will continue to live and prosper in the community that is Gonzaga.

4. My deepest hope and desire is that, regardless of where I am, I will always commit myself to one of the Jesuit ideals I was taught here at Gonzaga: to serve those people of the world who need our time, support, and energy most.

Jen Forsman

1. I have been *so* blessed during my years at Gonzaga. Being an AGAPE team leader helped me to look at my future in ways I have never before considered, and serving on SEARCH helped me to truly understand the meaning and value of service to God through service to others.

2. The two things I wish I would have participated in at GU are the Ignatian Retreat and Mission: Possible. Everyone always has such powerful experiences and I'm sad that I missed "both."

3. Graduation is scary. It's scary because in today's world, there is so much uncertainty. A few short weeks ago, we were at war. But easy isn't what GU has prepared us for – the world is what we have been preparing for over the last four years.

4. Gonzaga strives to create "men and women for others," and what an impressive goal that is! I must admit, as my time at GU comes to an end, I am not eager to make a lot of money. I'm eager to make a difference. If I can do that, then my GU experience – even the huge amount of debt I've accumulated – will all be worth it.

Doug Simmons

1. I believe the greatest blessing in time at Gonzaga was the chance to have Fr. Mike Treleaven in my life. He inspired me to achieve great things and to be a stronger Catholic through his constant statements of support and belief in my abilities.

2. I only wish that I had a chance to volunteer my time with the Campus Kids program. I wish I could have been that voice for at least one of them.

3. I'm concerned about the possibility of being deployed to the Middle East. My hope is that the service which I will gladly render to my country only makes me a better Christian and member of this world.

4. After attending the AGAPE retreat back in my sophomore year I have been working on allowing myself to accept the fact that God loves me in all that I do. I hope I might serve as a guide for others lost or at least doubting while they serve in the Army. Faith is important for everyone, even for soldiers who sometimes have nothing else to see them through.

†

I don't know what themes you heard in these testimonies but I hear the ideals of faith in God, commitment to service, gratitude for gifts received, dedication to friendships, and ideals – high ideals – which are not in any way "corny" but come from the deepest part of the human heart where God inspires us to have great dreams.

A defining moment in these last four years was the evening of September 11th, when we, like millions of Americans all over the country, gathered to pray. We gathered by the hundreds with our candles on the steps of the Crosby Student Center. We prayed for those who were tragically killed, we prayed for peace, some worried for friends and family in lower Manhattan they had not heard from. We sang. We cried. Many carried American Flags. On arguably the most tragic day in American history a moment in time that will shape us as profoundly as the Civil War, we were in shock, yes, but we stood with each other in hope. We knew that we were united with each other by God's love and that God would help us. We also felt a deep love for the great ideals we learned here at Gonzaga and on which our country is founded. In the months that followed, we knew in our hearts what makes a life successful. We saw it displayed in the willing sacrifice of women and men of simplicity and nobility: our police and firefighters. How easy it is to forget what we knew to be true so clearly then.

There are no guarantees for what lay ahead of us individually or as a nation. We have no guarantees about the economy, about an end of terrorism or safety from global disease. And we live in a time when two-thirds of the world's Christians live in countries where they face the threat of persecution and death for their commitment to the Gospel message. But we know from our own experience that the most tragic times can bring out the best in the human heart – a heart made in the likeness of God's own. And we believe that even in the face of these uncertainties, that commitment to great ideals – to *love* – is the *only* path to hope.

One week before the first Battle of Bull Run where he was killed, Sullivan Ballou, a major in the Second Rhode Island Volunteers, wrote home to his wife in Smithfield:

July 14, 1861 Washington, DC

Dear Sarah, the indications are very strong that we shall move in a few days, perhaps tomorrow. Unlest I should not be able to write you again, I feel impelled to write a few lines that may fall under your eye when I am no more.

I have no misgivings about, or lack of confidence in the cause in which I am engaged, and my courage does not halt or falter. I know how American civilization now leans upon the triumph of the government and how great a debt we owe to those who went before us through the blood and suffering of the revolution. And I am willing, perfectly willing, to lay down all my joys in this life to help...pay that debt.

Sarah, my love for you is deathless. It seems to bind me with mighty cables that nothing but omnipotence can break. And yet my love of country comes over me like a strong wind and bears me irresistibly with all those chains to the battlefield.

The memory of all the blissful moments I have enjoyed with you come crowding over me, and I feel most deeply grateful, to God, and you, that I have enjoyed them for so long. And how hard it is for me to give them up and burn to ashes the hopes and future years, when God willing we might still have lived and loved together and see our boys grown up to honorable manhood around us.

If I do not return, my dear Sarah, never forget how much I loved you-nor that when my last breath escapes me on the battlefield, it will whisper your name. Forgive my many faults and the many pains I have caused you. How thoughtless, how foolish I have sometimes been. But oh, Sarah, if the dead can come back to this earth, and flit unseen around those they love, I shall always be with you in the brightest day and the darkest night. Always. Always. And when the soft breeze fans your cheek, it shall be my breath, or the cool air on your throbbing temple, it shall be my spirit passing by. Sarah, do not mourn me dead. Think I am gone, and wait for me, for we shall meet again.

My friends, as Fr. Kolvenbach hopes, may you find ideals and dreams that are worthy of your life's commitment and sacrifice like Sullivan and Sarah his beloved. May you open yourselves to love that is worth your dying or a cause that can claim the ultimate sacrifice – the gift of your spirit and life. Then you shall be "successful" and find the happiness that even today you may still search to discover.

You leave us today. You are welcome to return: to rest, to retreat or to share with us your triumphs and your stories of love and commitment to values worth your life's energy. You are welcome to return. Always. Always.

On your journey don't surrender your dreams of love and justice. They are not corny. *They are from God* and are guaranteed to one day reach their fulfillment by Him who died for us and whose victory we celebrate today. And should we not meet again in this life, we shall wait for each other, for the Eucharist we share is His promise that we *shall* meet again.

So do not be afraid or allow your hearts to be troubled. Trust the peace that God gives when you dream and desire for high ideals of love: to be women and men for others. And know that God, who is love, mercy, and forgiveness, never leaves your side. His love for you is deathless. He shall always be with us in the brightest day and the darkest night. Always. Always. Always.

People of the Promise – The People of Great Hopes and Great Dreams

Christmas Eve Vigil Mass 2003
Cathedral of Our Lady of Lourdes

The Gospel of Matthew for tonight's Christmas Vigil Mass begins with a genealogy (1:1-17). The structure of the genealogy highlights the emphasis on kingship. Through the genealogy, Matthew tells the story of Israel – her origin, her kings, her exiles, and her fulfillment in the coming of the Messiah, and leaves us in no doubt concerning the identity of Jesus. He is the Messiah, the son of David, the son of Abraham. The latter two titles link Jesus to God's two great promises to Israel. "Son of David" recalls God's promise to raise up David's seed and establish his kingdom forever (2 Sam. 7:12-16). "Son of Abraham" recalls God's promise that Abraham's seed would be a blessing to the nations (Gen. 22:18). Both of these things – Messianic kingship and Gentile blessing – climax in the final pronouncement in Matthew's Gospel: "All authority has been given to me in heaven and earth [kingship]. Go therefore and make disciples of all the nations [Gentile blessing]…" (Matt. 28:18-19). The second reading from Acts records Paul's early preaching to indicate that the Chosen People were promised a Savior from the kingly line of David:

Then he removed Saul and raised up David as king;
of him he testified,
'I have found David, son of Jesse, a man after my own heart;
he will carry out my every wish.'
From this man's descendants God, according to his promise,
has brought to Israel a savior, Jesus.

The first reading from Isaiah announces the Promised One who will save Israel not only from her external enemies, but also from her own infidelity to the Covenant. Isaiah proclaims:

No more shall people call you "Forsaken,"
or your land "Desolate,"

but you shall be called "My Delight,"
and your land "Espoused."

Do you feel joy in this Christmas time as believers in God? Do you feel joy in the fact that the promised Messiah, the promised of David's line, the fulfillment of Israel's prophets and of the original covenant to Abraham, has been born? If you are having difficulty in feeling the joy this feast and this season "should" elicit in your heart, maybe it is because you need to explore more deeply exactly what God's promise means to the people of Israel, to the Christian Church, the family of all humankind, and to each of us as individuals and members of families.

To do this, let us recall the anointing of King David by God, who was deemed the favored one in the Book of Samuel. Once in power however, we remember David's great sin recorded by the Prophet Nathan:

Chapter 12

1 And the LORD sent Nathan to David. He came to him, and said to him, "There were two men in a certain city, the one rich and the other
poor. 2 The rich man had very many flocks and herds; 3 but the poor
man had nothing but one little ewe lamb, which he had bought. And he brought it up, and it grew up with him and with his children; it used to eat of his morsel, and drink from his cup, and lie in his bosom, and it
was like a daughter to him. 4 Now there came a traveler to the rich
man, and he was unwilling to take one of his own flock or herd to prepare for the wayfarer who had come to him, but he took the poor
man's lamb, and prepared it for the man who had come to him." 5 Then
David's anger was greatly kindled against the man; and he said to Nathan, "As the LORD lives, the man who has done this deserves to
die; 6 and he shall restore the lamb fourfold, because he did this thing, and because he had no pity."

7 Nathan said to David, "**You are the man.** Thus says the LORD, the God of Israel, 'I anointed you king over Israel, and I delivered you out
of the hand of Saul; 8 and I gave you your master's house, and your master's wives into your bosom, and gave you the house of Israel and
of Judah; and if this were too little, I would add to you as much more. 9
Why have you despised the word of the LORD, to do what is evil in his sight? You have smitten Uriah the Hittite with the sword, and have

taken his wife to be your wife, and have slain him with the sword of the Ammonites. 10 Now therefore the sword shall never depart from your house, because you have despised me, and have taken the wife of Uriah the Hittite to be your wife.' 11 Thus says the LORD, 'Behold, I will raise up evil against you out of your own house; and I will take your wives before your eyes, and give them to your neighbor, and he shall lie with your wives in the sight of this sun. 12 For you did it secretly; but I will do this thing before all Israel, and before the sun.'" 13 David said to Nathan, "I have sinned against the LORD." And Nathan said to David, "The LORD also has put away your sin; you shall not die. 14 Nevertheless, because by this deed you have utterly scorned the LORD, the child that is born to you shall die."

If we can translate the horror of what David, the anointed one did, we might see it in today's news as these possible headlines:

God's favorite king in illicit affair!

Hero of Israel implicated in adultery and murder!

King David steals general's wife then has him executed!

And David's behavior in light of his anointing was emblematic for the whole of the Chosen people of God. Infidelity, scandal, blasphemy, moral and political corruption. This is the people and this is the royal line that Jesus chose to be descended from and "born into." This shocking reality perhaps can only be fully felt if we imagine that Jesus chooses to be born in each one of us individually in spite of our sinfulness, shames and failures, in our families with all of their hopes and shadows, in our world with all of its violence and terror, in our Church with both its timidity and public failures. This is what "should" be the cause of our inexpressible hope and joy tonight. Jesus chooses to be born into our lost innocence, our dashed hopes, or personal, familial, ecclesiastical mess-ups, in order to redeem us. Only if we allow ourselves to feel the weight of the history "*against any hope that god would be faithful to us because of our failures*" can we feel what the Christmas Carol *O Holy Night* expresses when it says:

O holy night, the stars are brightly shining
It is the night of our dear Savior's birth.
Long lay the world in sin and error pining,

Till he appeared and the soul felt its worth.
The thrill of hope, the weary world rejoices,
For yonder breaks a new and glorious morn.
Fall on your knees,
Oh, hear the angel voices
O night divine,
O night when Christ was born

Christmas' delights bring joy to children who are still innocent. This is obvious to each of us. But more than this, it should also bring joy to individuals, families, the Church and world – all who have long lost their innocence. Our failures did not merit God abandoning us, but merited for us his birth into our lost innocence so, as the song says, the "soul can feel its worth." In order to feel the true joy of Christmas, we need to allow ourselves to feel where we have lost hope in our lives, our families, our Church and our world. And we need to remember that it is into the weariness of these problems that Jesus *desires* to be born to renew in us as people of the promise, as people of great dreams, that sure and true hope that our salvation is here.

Jesus, you call us to faith that we may see your wonder and feel your presence. Help us where we have grown weary and where we have lost hope. Give us faith and show us anew that your love transcends our weaknesses and failures. The star of Christmas marks your coming. Christmas is ever near. The light of your presence in spite of the darkness in our world grows ever brighter. May our faith in you grow more powerful as well. In this faith, brings us the joy *of Christmas.*

Finding A True Voice

Fourth Sunday of Easter
Gonzaga University
Senior Mass, May 2, 2004

This Mass on the last Sunday of the school year is usually dedicated to the graduating Senior Class. So seniors, I ask you, "What have you learned in your four years here at Gonzaga?" The standard comment we hear at this time of year is that "I learned more outside the classroom than inside it. It is obvious why this is the case. Most of us are more geared toward relationships – the friends, roommates, faculty, chaplains, staff are what make the lasting impression - Even the Round the World Event yesterday. You know, I was dropping off my laundry at Clark's on Mission and I saw all these green shirts at a house on Sinto and Hamilton – I thought to myself: "Is this a CCASL project fixing up a house?" Then as I got closer I realized is it was a bunch of GU students themselves getting fixed! I later learned that the Spokane Police got involved as well.

Even this event will be remembered less for its "eventness" than for those friends you shared it with – even with the tazers – that is…*if* you can remember who you shared it with.

But what have you learned at GU these past years? Have you learned to be at rest – to enjoy leisure and reflection – I don't mean having a good time or knowing how to party well or "party hard." I mean to be at a peaceful rest and a moment of leisure – to listen deeply to your spirit and human experience? Have you learned to discern in your heart and head a true voice from a false one?

Our word for *school* from the ancient Greek means, literally, leisure. Josef Pieper in his landmark essay "Leisure as the Basis of Culture," points out that for the Greeks the word that means "Not Leisure" connotes the world of everyday work, not just the hustle and bustle of daily life but work itself. In our modern day, we might call that "not leisure" the world of play hard and party hard – the world we might have come to associate with life as a student in college.

It is really hard to be at leisure today – to listen and to reflect deeply on our human experience and our experience as spiritual beings. Everything seems to mitigate against it. Quite frankly, we are not rewarded for learning how just to "*be*." Raymond Reyes is fond of saying, "We are not 'Human Doings' but 'Human Beings.'" But just *being* is really hard. It is scary in fact.

Pieper is convinced that the world of total work "total play hard and party hard" is "pushing into history with a monstrous momentum." He says that we "are almost inclined, rightly or wrongly, to speak of a demonic power in history." What Pieper wants is leisure. "Not merely a little portion of rest on Sunday, but rather a whole preserve of true, unconfined humanity: a space of freedom, of true learning, of attunement to the world as a whole." Since he points out that the whole of western culture is built upon this leisure and time of rest, that if we can't reclaim, he believes we will destroy ourselves and our culture – that we will become victims of a slave state. He wrote his essay in the mid 1940s. I don't know about you, but I don't think we have reclaimed that notion of leisure.

The reason I begin with this reflection is because our readings today speak about our capacity to listen, to hear, and to receive Good News of eternal life. Paul and Barnabas in our first reading are sharing the Good News with fellow Jews in a synagogue on the Sabbath. Paul you will remember was the one who used to persecute the Church. He was convinced of the truth of his actions but God intervened in his life and opened up his heart and his capacity to hear more deeply a truth he could not reach with his own power. Convinced now of Jesus' Messiah-ship, he is speaking words that he has come to believe will lead people to eternal life. Many in this account from the Acts did not open their hearts to hear this good news but those who did rejoiced in the message they heard. Others sought to keep Paul and Barnabas from sharing the news and even desired to prevent people from hearing it.

In the Gospel today, Jesus too, speaks about listening and hearing. His sheep listen to Him and follow Him and He promises eternal life. It is important to know something about sheep lest we think that Jesus wants dumb mindless followers – a bunch of stupid sheep. We can get the wrong impression unless we know the relationship between sheep and shepherds.

Ten years ago I spent a year in sheep country in Northern Ireland. One day on Achill Island over Easter Weekend, Sean Grogin who lived next door, went to round up his sheep. Driving his old pickup that had a bad set of leaf springs on the rear of the truck, the sound of the springs creaking on the truck announced two miles off the approach of their shepherd. They instinctively started down the mountain toward where they knew the truck would stop. So based on this, the point Jesus is trying to make has to do with the keenness of our hearing the right shepherd, the right message, the truth He comes to share. Jesus does not want a herd mentality or an unreflective pack of animals following Him.

Our capacity to listen for the truth about life and the truth about God, and the message that can lead to eternal life is really the only important thing in the world. We each know how difficult it can be to listen honestly to our lives. We can listen honestly and know what the right thing is and still not do it. How amazing is the human mind and heart.

God knows how hard it is for us to listen honestly and even when we do, to act rightly in the face of the truth we know will make us happy and lead us to a meaningful life – an eternal life.

But God does give us the capacity to ask for help and God does promise to answer those cries for help when we make them.

What have you learned in college? Have you learned to be at leisure? Have you learned to listen deeply to your heart? If not, there is still time to know that the God of life is trying 24-7 to get through to you with a message that can lead you to eternal life. God does not just want you to work hard and party hard. God wants to give you *rest for your souls*. His yolk is easy and his burden is light. If you find yourself tired now or in the future and not fulfilled, don't be afraid to cry out for help. Listen deeply and know that God will find a way to answer your prayer.

Pieper himself said that culture would ultimately be saved by leisure. But as he points out, in the ancient world, festival is the heart of leisure and the very heart of festival is worship. And at the heart of worship is sacrifice. He says that "worship itself is a given – or it does not exist at all. For Christians, this is self-evident: that, after Christ, there is only one true and finally valid form of cultic worship, which is the sacramental Sacrifice of the Christian Church."

Seniors, I offer this Sacrifice of Worship for you and your future lives – that you find a way to listen deeply to that voice of God that calls you to a meaningful life – to an eternal life. I pray that you be "taken ultimately from the toil of the workday, to an endless day of celebration; to be rapt from the confines of the working environment into the very center of the world." This is your calling and this is the promise made by God to each of you from the very foundation of the world. It is your inheritance as baptized members of your Church. It is THE Good News that grounds everything for which our Church and University stands.

May God Bless you today and every day of your lives.

Finding Perfection in Body and Soul

Mass of the Holy Spirit
Gonzaga University
September 14, 2004
St. Aloysius Church

Have you ever watched the shows *Body Work* or *The Swan*? Perhaps one night channel surfing you stopped to watch *Nip and Tuck*. You might even arrange your evening with friends to watch *Extreme Makeovers*. Plastic surgery shows make up one of the fastest growing segments of reality TV. It seems lots of Americans are tuning in. Because it is not just aging female Boomers who are nipping and tucking or getting extreme makeovers, but so are male Boomers and teenagers – people ages 8-80. If I wanted a medical career and my main goal was to make a lot of money, I know what branch of medicine I would choose!

One can negatively view the growth market for plastic surgery in the U.S., and the reality TV shows that highlight the trend, as a sign that our culture is *just obsessed* with youth and beauty. While this may be the case, I prefer to see in the trend a spiritual desire for perfection *seeking a physical expression* that is good and God-given and grounded in the very soul of every person. The *challenge* of the individual *and* the culture is to properly discern not only the *source* of this desire for beauty and perfection, but how to cooperate with the author of the desire so that our choices and actions will bring true, lasting satisfaction, beauty and healing, not just to the body, but to the soul which is eternal.

As we commence our academic year we consciously remember that we share in the soul-grounded quest for perfection in beauty, truth, love and justice – a spiritual desire that seeks expression in a concrete educational mission and institution. As a community invited into the life of the Spirit, we too are called to a continual spiritual discernment on how best to act on these God-given dreams for our work as a university that is Jesuit/Catholic/Humanistic. Our hope in opening the academic year with a Mass of the Holy Spirit is to ask the Spirit for aid and guidance in our ongoing conversations and discernment of this mission. For the fulfillment of our deepest hopes and dreams for *this* university can only be realized by the blessing and assistance that comes from our individual and corporate *active* cooperation with the Spirit of God.

Our three readings today provide some substance for our reflection and give us things for which we can ask God's help.

1. Paul's exhortation to the community in Rome reminds us that we need to listen deeply to distinguish between the spirit that brings fear, death and enslavement and the Spirit that can give life and freedom – making us not only heirs of God but co-heirs with Christ in His mission.

   Do we excel as a community in providing the resources, encouragement and rewards necessary to engage the contemplative tradition that grounds university education not only as a secular enterprise, but as a spiritual endeavor in the Ignatian tradition? What definitions of success do we model and what help do we provide in aiding individuals (students, faculty and staff) to choose research, vocations, and careers that will feed the soul *and* feed the planet? How do we counter a culture that appears to reward, in the words of St. Paul, the unspiritual things that don't please God and promote instead a culture that rewards individuals moved by God's Spirit, *and how do we discern between the two?* In 1975 Fr. Arrupe, the Jesuit General said: *"We cannot be satisfied with an education which forms in our students an individualistic ideal of personal achievement, capable of opening the way to a brilliant personal life. We must form......a new mentality with new dynamic ideals which are based on the Gospel with all its consequences. [A Planet to Heal p. 241]"*

   Do we need a *Nip and Tuck* or an *Extreme Makeover*? These are matters for our communal discernment and things for which we can ask the Spirit's guidance.

2. Paul's letter to the Church in Corinth reminds us that each of us – from the first-year student to Jesuit rector and president, from the housekeeper to the department chair, from the newly appointed faculty member to the Trustee – each of us has been given particular and unique gifts *but* by the same Spirit. As an institution with many parts and persons, we are called to be united as one

body on a common mission a common mission that is more than a good or great university, but an exciting *even revolutionary force for change in the world.* A university as a united body *can achieve* this great mission when the Spirit energizes, animates and unites all we do.

What steps are we taking to find unity of purpose in a common mission? Have we seriously engaged the unique missions given to the Jesuit university by both the Society of Jesus and the Church? Based on the current Jesuit General Fr. Kolvenbach's recent exhortation, are we striving to *think and feel* with the Church – indeed loving the Church with all it faults and problems? Are we vigilant in identifying the ***constant pressures*** in a university to build individual kingdoms of schools or programs and working instead to achieve fruitful interdisciplinary cooperation for the success of all?

In the late 1980s Jesuits and companions at our university in El Salvador were murdered for fidelity to an educational mission that challenged the dominant culture of violence in their country. In our *own* day and cultural context, are there issues of faith and justice we as university are called to champion even if they might create a situation of threat or danger? Do we need a *Nip and Tuck* or an *Extreme Makeover*? These are issues for our ongoing conversation and things for which we can ask the Spirit's assistance.

3. In our Gospel from John, we remember that the Spirit of Christ and the Father anchor the Church's foundation. *The very gift of the Spirit that forms the first community* of believers is *inextricably* bound up with the mission of forgiveness, won for us by Christ in his life, passion, death and resurrection. How keenly Christ understood that the body of Christ on earth would need the power of the Spirit to do what they could not accomplish on their own – offer love and forgiveness. The signature characteristic of the early Christian community was how they loved one another. And where two or three are gathered you have Christ, but you will also have the constant need to forgive as the glue to keep the community healthy and the mission fruitful.

The academy has been described by both comedian and philosopher as more contentious than either the corporate world or the political arena. And if this is true, and I believe it is, it is *because* of our mission *as* a university. For we must debate and discern truth from falsehood, human progress from progressive decline, culture of life from culture of death, technological innovation from destabilizing invention, economic gain in the first world from global needs in the developing (world), dogmatic faith from false gods, and every other topic under the sun that is necessarily connected to ultimate meaning and human flourishing. It is a noble vocation. And as a community grounded in the Spirit, we have a higher calling on how we discuss issues that can create tensions and misunderstanding. We have a higher calling that can help us discern truth more clearly *and* more quickly because of how we treat each other.

How well do we honor the dignity and personhood of those we talk to or talk about – to base our judgments of ideas and persons on facts? Do we believe that progress in our discussions will be more successful if we ground ourselves in Christian charity? As my novice master Gordon Moreland use to say, there is a difference between being brutally frank and frankly brutal. How good are we at allowing the truth of the other to emerge even when it might challenge our intellectual theories, deeply held convictions, and beliefs? How readily do we forgive when we have made a mistake or hurt another person? From the outside looking in, do people know us mostly from our love of each other or from our intrigue? Do we need a *Nip and Tuck* or an *Extreme Makeover*? All are matters for our ongoing communal discernment and things for which we can ask the Spirit's guidance and help.

As a community and as a university, we can never say we have accomplished our Catholic, Jesuit or Humanistic mission. We are always pilgrims on the way, and to be honest, we are pilgrims who can lose our way. And as a work in progress and a pilgrim community striving for more authentic expressions of a university, Jesuit, Catholic and Humanistic, we should remind ourselves that our local conversations on these issues have a long history.

In 1977 a student wrote a letter to the Gonzaga Bulletin: *"Gonzaga as a Christian, Catholic, and Jesuit educational institution seems to be struggling to clarify its goals – goals which need to inspire the hearts and minds of [zealous] Christians like...myself." But let us not be too critical of this lack of direction, for the Church, the Society [of Jesus], [and]the laity.........from which institutions (such as) [like] Gonzaga gain their direction, are struggling to meet Christ in the modern world. When we discover more definitively our modern identity in terms of the service of faith and the promotion of justice, the institution in turn, will be imbued with the identity of our own lives and once again a specific direction will be gained. When this happens, we may find ourselves engaged in activities much more challenging and controversial than B-1[bomber] marches and lettuce boycotts."* That student was me.

Our consolation today and our reason for this Mass is that we *have* the option of inviting the Spirit of God *into our midst*. This makes us a *community of hope*. Whether we need a *Nip and Tuck* or an *Extreme Makeover*, as a community open to the Spirit there will never be any cost or co-pay required. All makeovers, *no matter how extreme*, are freely accomplished by the power of the Spirit. The only thing required of us is to be honest in our ongoing discernment and sincere and humble in asking the Spirit to accomplish what is impossible for us to accomplish on our own. For Christ desires that we succeed and longs to praise the Father for what *this* community accomplished *in His name* and *for His Kingdom*.